O Thou Kind Lord!

O Thou Kind Lord!

Prayers & Readings
for Children from
the Bahá'í Writings

Baha'i
Publishing
Trust

Contents

O Thou kind Lord!
Graciously bestow
a pair of heavenly wings
unto each of these fledglings
and give them spiritual power . . .

'Abdu'l-Bahá

Morning

Praise be unto Thee, O My God, that we have wakened to the splendours of the light of Thy Knowledge.

Bahá'u'lláh

Morning

I have wakened in Thy
shelter, O my God, and it
becometh him that seeketh
that shelter to abide within
the Sanctuary of Thy
protection and the
Stronghold of Thy defence.

Morning

Illumine my inner being,
O my Lord, with the
splendours of the Day-Spring
of Thy Revelation, even as
Thou didst illumine my outer
being with the morning light
of Thy favour.

Bahá'u'lláh

Growing and learning

O my Lord! O my Lord! I am a child of tender years. Nourish me from the breast of Thy mercy, train me in the bosom of Thy love, educate me in the school of Thy guidance and develop me under the shadow of Thy bounty.

'Abdu'l-Bahá

Growing and learning

O Lord! Make this youth radiant, and confer Thy bounty upon this poor creature. Bestow upon him knowledge, grant him added strength at the break of every morn and guard him within the shelter of Thy protection so that he may be freed from

error, may devote himself to
the service of Thy Cause, may
guide the wayward, lead the
hapless, free the captives and
awaken the heedless, and
that all may be blessed with
Thy remembrance and praise.
Thou art the Mighty and the
powerful.

'Abdu'l-Bahá

Protection

O God, guide me, protect me,
make of me a shining lamp
and a brilliant star. Thou art
the Mighty and the Powerful.

'Abdu'l-Bahá

Protection

I am, O my God, but a tiny
seed which Thou hast sown in
the soil of Thy love, and
caused to spring forth by the
hands of Thy bounty. This
seed craveth, therefore, in its
inmost being, for the waters
of Thy mercy and the living
fountain of Thy grace.

Protection

Send down upon it, from the
heaven of Thy loving-
kindness, that which will
enable it to flourish beneath
Thy shadow and within
the borders of Thy court.

Bahá'u'lláh

Protection

I have risen this morning by
Thy grace, O my God, and left
my home trusting wholly in
Thee, and committing myself
to Thy care. Send down, then,
upon me, out of the heaven
of Thy mercy, a blessing from
Thy side, and enable me to

Protection

return home in safety even as
Thou didst enable me to set
out under Thy protection
with my thoughts fixed
steadfastly upon Thee.

There is none other God
but Thee, the One, the
Incomparable, the All-
Knowing, the All-Wise.

Bahá'u'lláh

Healing

If an animal be sick, let the children try to heal it, if it be hungry, let them feed it, if thirsty, let them quench its thirst, if weary, let them see that it rests.

'Abdu'l-Bahá

Healing

Thy Name is my healing, O
my God, and remembrance of
Thee is my remedy. Nearness
to Thee is my hope, and love
for Thee is my companion.
Thy mercy to me is my

Healing

healing and my succour in both this world and the world to come. Thou, verily, art the All-Bountiful, the All-Knowing, the All-Wise.

Bahá'u'lláh

Help from God

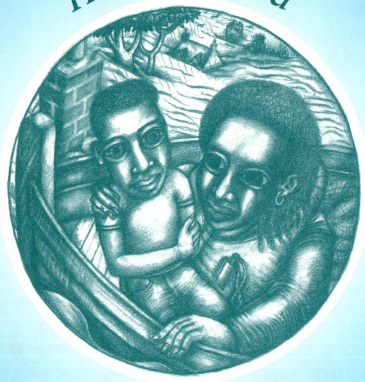

Be assured that the eye of His loving-kindness is directed towards thee and the glance of His mercifulness resteth upon thee.

'Abdu'l-Bahá

Help from God

Is there any Remover of difficulties save God? Say: Praised be God! He is God! All are His servants, and all abide by His bidding!

The Báb

Help from God

Remember not your own limitations; the help of God will come to you. Forget yourself. God's help will surely come!

'Abdu'l-Bahá

Home and family

O Lord, forgive us, and our fathers and mothers and fulfil whatsoever we have desired from the ocean of Thy grace and Divine generosity.

Bahá'u'lláh

Home and family

O my God! Let the outpourings of Thy bounty and blessings descend upon homes whose inmates have embraced Thy Faith, as a token of Thy grace and as a mark of Thy loving-kindness from Thy presence.

The Báb

Home and family

. . . every home where God is
praised and prayed to, and
His Kingdom proclaimed, that
home is a garden of God and
a paradise of His happiness.

'Abdu'l-Bahá

The earth

So powerful is the light of unity that it can illuminate the whole earth.

Bahá'u'lláh

The earth

Blessed is the spot, and the house, and the place, and the city, and the heart, and the mountain, and the refuge, and the cave, and the valley, and the land, and the sea, and the island, and the meadow where mention of God hath been made, and His praise glorified.

Bahá'u'lláh

The earth

The earth is but one country, and mankind its citizens.

Bahá'u'lláh

The world, our family

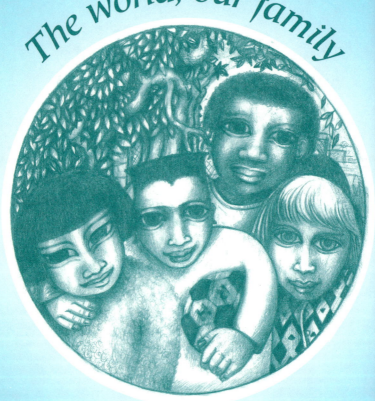

Let your heart burn with loving kindness for all who may cross your path.

'Abdu'l-Bahá

The world, our family

O Thou kind Lord! Unite all.
Let the religions agree and
make the nations one, so that
they may see each other as
one family and the whole
earth as one home. May they
all live together in perfect
harmony.

'Abdu'l-Bahá

The world, our family

God grant that the light of
unity may envelop the whole
earth, and that the seal, 'The
Kingdom is God's', may be
stamped upon the brow of all
its peoples.

Bahá'u'lláh

Guiding others

Strive that your actions day by day may be beautiful prayers.

'Abdu'l-Bahá

Guiding others

Pray to God that He may strengthen you in divine virtue, so that you may be as angels in the world, and beacons of light to disclose the mysteries of the Kingdom to those with understanding hearts.

'Abdu'l-Bahá

Guiding others

O God, my God! Aid Thou Thy trusted servants to have loving and tender hearts. Help them to spread, amongst all the nations of the earth, the light of guidance that cometh from the Company on High.

'Abdu'l-Bahá

Love the creatures for the sake of God and not for themselves. You will never become angry or impatient if you love them for the sake of God. Humanity is not perfect. There are imperfections in every human being and you will always become unhappy if you look toward the people themselves. But if you look

Guiding others

toward God you will love
them and be kind to them,
for the world of God is the
world of perfection and
complete mercy. Therefore do
not look at the shortcomings
of anybody; see with the
sight of forgiveness.

'Abdu'l-Bahá

The 19 Day Feast

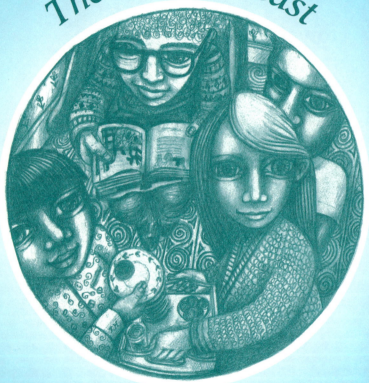

You must continue to keep the Nineteen Day Feast. It is very important; it is very good.

'Abdu'l-Bahá

O God! Dispel all those
elements which are the cause
of discord, and prepare for us
all those things which are the
cause of unity and accord.
O God! Descend upon us
Heavenly Fragrance and
change this gathering into a

The 19 Day Feast

gathering of Heaven! Grant to us every benefit and every food. Prepare for us the Food of Love! Give to us the Food of Knowledge! Bestow upon us the Food of Heavenly Illumination!

'Abdu'l-Bahá

Consultation

The light of truth shineth
from the faces of those who
engage in consultation.

'Abdu'l-Bahá

Consultation

In all things it is necessary to consult . . . it is and will always be a cause of awareness and of awakening and a source of good and well-being.

Bahá'u'lláh

Consultation

. . . consultation causeth the living waters to flow in the meadows of man's reality, the rays of ancient glory to shine upon him, and the tree of his being to be adorned with wondrous fruit.

'Abdu'l-Bahá

New Year

The new year hath appeared and the spiritual springtime is at hand.

'Abdu'l-Bahá

New Year

Praised be Thou, O my God, that Thou hast ordained Naw-Rúz as a festival unto those who have observed the Fast for love of Thee . . .

Bahá'u'lláh

New Year

If we are not happy and joyous at this season, for what other season shall we wait and for what other time shall we look?

'Abdu'l-Bahá

53

Evening

O my God, my Master, the Goal of my desire! This, Thy servant seeketh to sleep in the shelter of Thy mercy, and to repose beneath the canopy of Thy grace, imploring Thy care and Thy protection.

Bahá'u'lláh

Evening

I have committed, O my Lord,
my spirit and my entire being
into the right hand of Thy
might and Thy protection,
and I lay my head on my
pillow through Thy power,

Evening

and lift it up according to Thy
will and Thy good pleasure.
Thou art, in truth, the
Preserver, the Keeper, the
Almighty, the Most Powerful.

'Abdu'l-Bahá

© 1993 Bahá'í Publishing Trust
27 Rutland Gate
London SW7 1PD

From a selection
by Anne Walker

Illustrations by Rob Hain
© Bahá'í Publishing Trust

British Library
Cataloguing-in-Publication Data

A catalogue record for this book is
available from the British Library

ISBN 1-870989-38-4